I SHALL NOT WANT

How to Destroy Lack and Poverty

by Michael Duever

Published by:
Duever House Publishing
P.O. Box 5921
Johnson City, TN 37602
www.Ishallnotwant.com

REVISED 2020
ISBN 9781098353865

Printed in the United States of America
For Worldwide Distribution

Table of Contents

Introduction

Proverbs 4:7
Wisdom is the principal thing; *therefore* get wisdom: and with all thy getting get understanding.

Psalm 23:1
The LORD *is* my shepherd; I shall not want.

Psalm 34:12-13
What man *is he that* desireth life, *and* loveth *many* days, that he may see good? Keep thy tongue from evil, and thy lips from speaking guile.

James 1:4
But let patience have *her* perfect work, that ye may be perfect and entire, wanting nothing.

Psalm 126:1-2
When the LORD turned again the captivity of Zion, we were like them that dream.
Then was our mouth filled with laughter, and our tongue with singing: then said they among the heathen, The LORD hath done great things for them.

Wisdom is the principal thing. Wisdom has been explained as knowing how to use knowledge at the right time and in the right place. And I asked the Lord for wisdom to help me get this revelation that He has shown me into a format that is easy to understand, so that even the person who may not have had prior knowledge about the power of words or the power of the tongue may read this book and put it into practice.

When a new concept or idea is introduced into society, it is often met with resistance. Change is not something we humans particularly like or run towards. When I have explained or tried to explain this revelation God has given me, resistance is often what I have met. A person I may be talking with may look at me and say to himself or herself, "Who is this person, and why should I believe him? I haven't seen him on TV!" But God even chooses to use the foolish things to confound the wise, doesn't He? Sometimes the simplest of things can be confusing to a grown man. When God showed me this revelation, for a long while afterwards I wondered why He chose to give it to me. I had never heard this from anyone before.

It is my prayer that this book will reveal to you a hidden mystery and secret that really is still unknown in the Christian world.

I believe that it is not by chance that you are reading this book, but that you picked up this book by divine appointment. I believe that the Holy Spirit has tilled the soil of your heart to hear, see, and understand this message. The title of this book may have piqued your interest and I believe that God had you pick this up, or perhaps someone you know told you to get this. Well, get ready for a change of thinking. When I would explain this revelation to people, I could actually *feel* it enter into them and go down inside, and it would either stay and they would understand and get totally excited, or else I would *sense* it come right back up and out and watch them look at me like a deer at headlights. That is when I began to understand that the Holy Spirit had to prepare people to hear. As it says in Ephesians: the eyes of your understanding being *enlightened*, I pray that the eyes of *your* understanding will be enlightened by the Holy Spirit.

The goal of this book is to show you that there is a Land of No Want, to show you what that means, and to show you that it is closer than you know and is a place that you can enter and live in. This book will cause you to laugh, for what will be revealed will sound foolish to the natural mind, but through the knowledge of God's Word, your mind will be renewed to think like God thinks. This will also expose the devil and his operations against your life.

And when you apply what you learn through this book, you will be able to destroy lack and poverty by stopping the devils operations against your life, with your tongue and your words.

Let's begin.

CHAPTER 1

The English Language

In the past when scholars translated the Bible from the original Hebrew and Greek, many times the real meaning was lost or covered up. At the time when the Bible was translated, many of those scholars added words to the translation to try to help us understand. This is why some of the true meanings of Scripture are lost in translation. The King James Bible remains the most well-known, truest and loved of all translations of the Word of God in the English language. Italicized words have been added in the KJV Bible to help us who read and speak English to understand more fully what is meant.

In English, we have only one word for love, which is, namely, *love*. Yet, in many other languages, there are several words that can be used to indicate different meanings of the word *love*, as in Greek. Greek has three words for love: *agape, philo,* and *eros.* All three words speak of love, but each has a distinct and unique assignment: to express an attribute of the word *love* that is different from the others.

So, we who use the English language have to add other words to the word *love* to aid in expressing different meanings. This is true for other words in our language as well.

An example in Scripture of where words were added (italicized) to bring out the intended meaning, is the following:

Malachi 3:10
Bring ye all the tithes into the storehouse, that there may be meat in mine house, and prove me now herewith, saith the LORD of hosts, if I will not open you the windows of heaven, and pour you out a blessing, that *there shall* not *be room* enough *to receive it.*

There is no place in the KJV Bible where more than three italicized words have been added in one sentence other than this verse. And look, it's a verse that deals with tithes. Money. Is there something hidden here? When the italicized words are taken out (which the translators put in to "help" give a clearer understanding),

Malachi 3:10 (b) becomes:
"...if I will not open you the windows of heaven and pour you out a blessing, *that not enough.*"

This now says something different. Tithes and offerings are two separate things, not just one, and offerings are necessary in addition to tithes to cause Luke 6:38 to work for you in the area of finances. Tithes open the windows of heaven and are just the beginning. Does "not having enough room" sound like a blessing? The added italicized words have created a different picture of what tithes do. I've lived in places where I didn't have enough room, and it wasn't because I was loaded with abundance; rather, it was due to lack. And as you read more of this book, you will understand that any lack of room is due to confessions that were made for it. I used to quote that I wouldn't have enough room, and I got it. I had faith for lack. Sounds crazy, I know, but when you know the truth, it will set you free. Some misunderstandings about tithes and offerings have occurred as well. Tithes belong to God. Offerings will cause a harvest. And having **more** than enough room will be an added blessing.

Luke 6:38
Give, and it shall be given unto you; good measure, pressed down, and shaken together, and run-

ning over, shall men give into your bosom. For with the same measure that ye mete withal it shall be measured to you again.

In the English language, many times one word inserted or used incorrectly (as in Malachi 3:10 above) can alter the true meaning of a statement and, as a result, misunderstanding can very well occur.

That is one reason why lawyers are hired: to read over documents and interpret to you and me *what the words are truly saying*. Think about that.

Let me pose a question: Would it be possible in our language that, under the guise of appearing right and sounding correct, we have in fact been taught to talk wrong? Could we be using words in our conversations daily that appear to be filled with life and good will, and sound correct, but in fact are filled with destruction?

For example, if words of love and appreciation (life) are spoken into a relationship, the relationship will blossom. If words of hate and dissatisfaction, predictions of divorce or separation, or other negative words are spoken over a relationship (words filled with death), then the relationship will disintegrate.

Confession does bring possession.

Where do these words that we speak come from? The answer lies in what a person has filled his or her heart with. Jesus said:

Matthew 12:34
    O generation of vipers, how can ye, being evil, speak good things? for out of the abundance of the heart the mouth speaketh.

And what is in the heart came in through the ears and eyes.

Are we using words in our conversations that appear to be filled with life? Many words that we use have meanings that are understood, and the usage of those words is correct. However, there are words being used, and certain words in particular, that mean something totally different from what they are thought to mean. And this, as you will see, is shocking.

Society has changed, for example, the implication of the word *gay* to mean homosexual. The word *gay* has not changed its meaning just because we use it to label a certain lifestyle. The definition of a word does not change just because the usage of that word changes. We can say it changes, but it doesn't. Now, with everyone in this country calling people who live this lifestyle "gay," then we are claiming that they are merry, cheerful, and jolly, as well as the other meanings of the word listed below, but *not* homosexual.

I've known some people in this lifestyle, and they do appear to be just that: gay. Now heterosexual people confess that they themselves are not gay. They are just confessing that they are *not* merry, cheerful, and jolly, thinking that they are telling people that they are not homosexual. Does this make sense to you?

Gay (ga) adj. gayer, gayest. 1. Showing or characterized by exuberance or mirthful excitement; merry; cheerful; jolly. 2. Bright or lively, especially in color. 3. Full of or given to social or other pleasures.

Remember the Flintstones' song "We'll Have a Gay Old Time"? The word is properly used.

Someone may say that definitions have changed over time and these new definitions are now acceptable, but this is a very serious statement, because words are spirit and eternal. They don't change, just like the real *Word*, Jesus. Jesus never changes. He's always the same.

Hebrews 13:8
   Jesus Christ the same yesterday, and to day, and for ever.

Psalm 89:34
   My covenant will I not break, nor alter the thing that is gone out of my lips.

When Adam named the animals and birds, God declared that their names would be whatever Adam called them and would not change. Words carry life or death and words do not lose their meaning due to time and/or cultural changes even though people use them differently. Some people joke around and say different things to make people laugh, and perhaps say "that looks bad" in slang, meaning "that's really good-looking." But using the word *bad* in that sentence doesn't change its real meaning. Isaiah the prophet gave us a warning:

Isaiah 5:20 (a)
   Woe unto them that call evil good, and good evil.

The chief point that I will make about the English language is that, under the influence of the prince of the power of the air, who is satan, we have been taught to talk wrong. Not only have we been taught to talk wrong, but we have also been very well trained to think that the way we talk is correct. Words have not lost their true meanings because of different usage. We have unknowingly used words that have created chaos in our own worlds, and caused undesired results and sometimes even destruction. We have used our own mouths against ourselves.

Ever hear someone say you are your own worst enemy? Well, you're not. The deceiver satan is, and he likes to get you to use your tongue against yourself.

Romans 12:2
And be not conformed to this world: but be ye transformed by the renewing of your mind, that ye may prove what *is* that good, and acceptable, and perfect will of God.

Have our minds been renewed? Is the Bible's use of words outdated? Often I have heard that the Bible, especially the King James Version, is hard to understand. Being trained by the world to talk and then reading the KJV Bible thus seems unfamiliar to present-day language and even appears outdated. Only after I was saved did I understand the Bible.

2 Corinthians 6:17 (a)
Wherefore come out from among them, and be ye separate, saith the Lord.

Our conversation language for the most part has been like that of the world, and by world, I mean the non-Christian world. We sound like, look like, and even act like the world, but as believers we are supposed to come out from among the world and be separate from them. This includes our conversation. In chapter 4, I shall show you the correct way to talk. It is opposite to the way of the world and foolishness to the mind, but it has results that you will like.

The truth was veiled from our eyes, but the Holy Spirit has revealed truth to teach us.

1 Corinthians 2:6-10

Howbeit we speak wisdom among them that are perfect: yet not the wisdom of this world, not of the princes of this world, that come to nought:

But we speak the wisdom of God in a mystery, *even* the hidden *wisdom*, which God ordained before the world unto our glory;

Which none of the princes of this world knew: for had they known *it*, they would not have crucified the Lord of glory.

But as it is written, Eye hath not seen, nor ear heard, neither have entered into the heart of man, the things which God hath prepared for them that love him.

But God hath revealed *them* unto us by his Spirit: for the Spirit searcheth all things, yea, the deep things of God.

What the Lord will reveal to you through this book has been hidden from us in the past.

1 Corinthians 2:14
But the natural man receiveth not the things of the Spirit of God: for they are foolishness unto him: neither can he know *them*, because they are spiritually discerned.

James 1:22
But be ye doers of the word, and not hearers only, deceiving your own selves.

Today will be a new day for you, a day when God teaches you how to talk correctly.

John 16:13 a
Howbeit when he, the Spirit of truth, is come, he will guide you into all truth.

What also will happen is that your image of God will be changed to see HIM as your provider and supplier of abundance. You'll see God is for you. Your thoughts are going to change as well and you're going to go on the offensive. You have the victory!

2 Corinthians 10:4-5
(For the weapons of our warfare *are* not carnal, but mighty through God to the pulling down of strongholds;)

Casting down imaginations, and every high thing that exalteth itself against the knowledge of God, and bringing into captivity every thought to the obedience of Christ.

Ephesians 3:20
Now unto him that is able to do exceeding abundantly above all that we ask or THINK, according to the power that worketh in us…

CHAPTER 2
Confession and the Tongue

Proverbs 16:23
The heart of the wise teacheth his mouth, and addeth learning to his lips.

Proverbs 13:14
The law of the wise *is* a fountain of life, to depart from the snares of death.

Proverbs 12:18
There is that speaketh like the piercings of a sword: but the tongue of the wise *is* health.

Proverbs 10:19
In the multitude of words there wanteth not sin: but he that refraineth his lips *is* wise.

Proverbs 18:21
Death and life *are* in the power of the tongue: and they that love it shall eat the fruit thereof.

Proverbs 21:23
    Whoso keepeth his mouth and his tongue, keepeth his soul from troubles.

Ephesians 4:29
    Let no corrupt communication proceed out of your mouth, but that which is good to the use of edifying, that it may minister grace unto the hearers.

The Bible has a lot to say about our tongue and how we use it. Proverbs considers a wise man to be very aware of the words he speaks and able to control them. (Man is both male and female) There is great teaching on the tongue and the power of it, and we must realize that we can bind things up or loose things into being with words. Picture binding up a bail of hay, versus cutting the twine and letting the hay go free. That's a little glimpse of the power we have with our tongue.

Matthew 18:18
    Verily I say unto you, Whatsoever ye shall bind on earth shall be bound in heaven; and whatsoever ye shall loose on earth shall be loosed in heaven.

The tongue has been and is being used to loose blessing and cursing, and many people have been cursed or blessed by other people or even by themselves. Your tongue can start a curse.

Jesus made a profound statement about the words we say with our mouths and how those words are powerful.

Mark 11:23
For verily I say unto you, That whosoever shall say unto this mountain, Be thou removed, and be thou cast into the sea; and shall not doubt in his heart, but shall believe that those things which he saith shall come to pass; he shall have whatsoever he saith.

Believe what you say shall come to pass, and you shall have whatsoever you say. That's a wonderful statement. We believe that most of the things we are saying are true, until the time when we are taught different or are proven wrong and then change our thinking, and at that point it is up to us to choose what to do with the new information. This book itself is presenting new information. Remember, we only know what we have been taught.

Hosea 4:6
My people are destroyed for lack of knowledge: because thou hast rejected knowledge, I will also reject thee, that thou shalt be no priest to me: seeing thou hast forgotten the law of thy God, I will also forget thy children.

Friends, let's embrace knowledge now, and as Proverbs 4:7 says, get wisdom and understanding, and also add learning to our lips so we can stop cursing ourselves.

Watch how God talked to the people in the Old Testament about their words.

Malachi 3:13
Your words have been stout against me, saith the LORD. Yet ye say, what have we spoken *so much* against thee?

Stout means to complain, contend, and debate. Words are important to God, so we should consider words to be important to us. Christianity itself has been called "The Great Confession."

To some of you, this is nothing new and you have heard these scriptures and read them many times. What we must realize is that we are creating our worlds around us with our words. And some of you do not like what has been created. Well, I've got *good news*. So fasten your spiritual belt because what you are going to learn here will take you out of those undesirable worlds.

The world you see today, that you are surrounded by and live in daily, has been created by the words that you spoke yesterday. We look at the world we created and may find ourselves wondering if our words really are powerful, and if they really work the way we've been taught. We've been watching our words and consider ourselves to be positive, and never really speak anything negative. But why aren't we getting the results we desire? For example, are you strapped for time and money? In other words, broke? That's an undesirable world that was created by words. Your words! Have you ever said you were strapped for time, or that your plate was full? And where did the saying "strapped for time" come from, and what have you spoken out about yourself? You may argue, "Well, I have to work long hours to make ends meet." Remember, this world is ruled by words. That's how God set up this system. He began by saying, "Let there be light: and there was light" (Genesis 1:3). And your words rule your world.

Proverbs 18:21
   Death and life *are* in the power of the tongue: and they that love it shall eat the fruit thereof.

Have we given up the faith that our words are important, and have we become relaxed and loose with our tongues? Are we saying things now that we wouldn't have dared to speak years ago, because we thought they were negative or a bad confession? Are we doing this because we have come to believe that words are really not all that powerful.

Let me make a small demonstration. The world was created when God spoke a word. Take the letter "l" out of *world* and you have *word*. Coincidence?

Hebrews 11:1-3
> Now faith is the substance of things hoped for, the evidence of things not seen.
> For by it the elders obtained a good report.
> Through faith we understand that the worlds were framed by the word of God, so that things which are seen were not made of things which do appear.

If you do not like the world you are living in, change the words you have been saying. It's up to you.

The book of James tells us that the tongue is like the rudder of a ship and that turning the rudder causes the ship to change direction. Changing the words, and especially now the usage of words, will change that rudder and will change your world. Give your words time to work. A big ship doesn't turn on a dime, especially if it has been going full steam ahead for many years.

James 3:4-6

Behold also the ships, which though *they be* so great, and *are* driven of fierce winds, yet are they turned about with a very small helm, whithersoever the governor listeth.

Even so the tongue is a little member, and boasteth great things. Behold, how great a matter a little fire kindleth!

And the tongue *is* a fire, a world of iniquity; so is the tongue among our members, that it defileth the whole body, and setteth on fire the course of nature; and it is set on fire of hell.

The tongue sets on *fire* the course of nature, or sets into motion the wheels of life! What wheels have you set into motion with your tongue?

Jesus never changes. His Word is still the same. He is the Word Himself. The answer is in Him and He has the words for you to say that will create a whole new world for you to live in.

Psalm 50:23

Whoso offereth praise glorifieth me: and to him that ordereth *his* conversation *aright* will I show the salvation of God.

We used to sing that verse of Scripture as a song in Canada. Not too many songs sung in church today are scripturally correct, but we must get back to that.

27

When we order our conversation aright, God will show *His salvation* here and now on planet earth for us! How many know that the word *salvation* includes much more than eternal life with Him?

In Hebrew, the word *salvation* comes from the word *yesha* or *yasha*, which means:

- liberty, deliverance, prosperity
- safety, salvation, saving
- aid, victory, prosperity, health, welfare
- to be open, wide, or free, to get victory

Does that sound good? Glory to God! Read that definition out loud right now. And God will show us liberty, deliverance, prosperity, and all good things.

Romans 10:10 (b)
   And with the mouth confession is made unto salvation.

Here we see that we use our words to bring in salvation, to bring in prosperity, to bring in health and victory. But there is a word that we have been using that has been creating the exact **opposite** of salvation in our lives. We have been blind to it, and it's a four-letter word.

Now, if we have been talking correctly, as we have believed, why don't we all have that salvation flowing in our lives? Realize that God is no respecter of persons, and *you* can change your words to create this salvation where it never existed before.

Matthew 12:37
For by thy words thou shalt be justified, and by thy words thou shalt be condemned.

The world's conversation is filled with covetousness and greed, and talking like the world creates dissatisfaction, frustration, and emptiness. Talking like God or quoting God's Word, however, brings peace, joy, contentment, and *yesha* (or salvation)!

Hebrews 13:5
Let your conversation *be* without covetousness; *and be* content with such things as ye have: for he hath said, I will never leave thee, nor forsake thee.

I heard one preacher say: "I am content with increase." Glory to God.

Why have we had so many problems with our tongues? Because our heads are getting in the way. Our thinking has been wrong, thus influencing our tongues. Have you ever heard that the battle is in the mind? When you put on the shield of faith to quench the fiery darts of the wicked one, where do you think those darts are aimed? At your chest? No! They are aimed at your tongue! Remember, the tongue is set on fire by hell! And those fiery darts are aimed at your tongue to try to set it on fire. But you don't have to let it. God said that out of your innermost being shall flow rivers of living water— and the water puts out the fire!

I'm going to show you where *you* have been fanning the fire, and show you how to put out that fire. Now, we can only put the blame on ourselves for using bad words, since we have the power and ability to control our tongues.

Isaiah 1:5
Why should ye be stricken any more? ye will revolt more and more: the whole head is sick, and the whole heart faint.

The whole head is sick, and the whole heart faint. It's time for healing! Hallelujah! The tongue will then get it too!

Here's something to think about. Jesus said these words:

Matthew 12:36

But I say unto you, That every idle word that men shall speak, they shall give account thereof in the day of judgment.

John 8:12

Then spake Jesus again unto them, saying, I am the light of the world: he that followeth me shall not walk in darkness, but shall have the light of life.

John 8:32

And ye shall know the truth, and the truth shall make you free.

CHAPTER 3

A Glorious Day

It happened one day as I was mowing the lawn at a friend's house. My friend Majesta called me up to the house where her mother, Kay, had stopped by to see her. Kay was planning to commit suicide that day. After a life of basic hell, even as a Christian, she could see no way out except suicide. Kay was planning to check out for good, but thank God, Kay is alive and very well today. We prayed with her, and as we did, we canceled and broke curses that were over her life. Curses from her ancestors, from her husband, from over her marriage, from a palm reader she once went to consult, and from herself. Blessings are now there in place of those curses, and Kay is finding out what life is really like.

As noted before, the topics of blessings and curses

are just being mentioned here, but are included in and are related to the subject of the tongue.

The Bible is true. Jesus was anointed of the Holy Spirit to preach the gospel to the poor. He was sent to heal the brokenhearted, to preach deliverance to the captives, and recovering of sight to the blind, to set at liberty them that are bruised, and to preach the acceptable year of the Lord. That is: Jubilee!! Which is: Let the oppressed go free. All debts canceled. Glory to God! And that's what happened to Kay that day. She was delivered. The Word set her free.

Now, a week or so after we had prayed and canceled curses from over Kay, the Holy Spirit spoke to her and said: "Never say 'want' again, nor 'need,' because need is worse." She proceeded to call me and tell me what had been spoken to her. She hung up the phone and there was an explosion inside of me as the Holy Spirit illuminated my understanding, and thus this book was written. Praise God! I will show you how Kay's own words kept her alive.

Kay is now enjoying a new abundant life and is changing the world around her by the words of her mouth.

John 10:10
    The thief cometh not, but for to steal, and to kill,
and to destroy: I am come that they might have life,
and that they might have *it* more abundantly.

In the Greek concordance, these last words "more abundantly" are translated: superabundantly (in quantity) or superior (in quality), to be in excess, excessive, exceeding abundantly above, beyond measure, more, extravagantly.

Also, Jesus knew who satan was, yet He didn't use the word "satan" here; He used the word "thief." Jesus called satan by name.

Luke 10:18-19
    And he said unto them, I beheld Satan as lightning
fall from heaven.
    Behold, I give you power to tread on serpents and
scorpions, and over all the power of the enemy; and
nothing shall by any means hurt you.

The word *thief* is not in that verse. Many people think that the thief spoken of in John 10:10 is satan, and speak out that the devil is coming to steal from, kill, and destroy them. What power are you giving to the devil? If you study this, the thief is not satan, but false teachers. Look at this:

John 10:8
All that ever came before me are thieves and robbers: but the sheep did not hear them.

The devil can't steal from me, kill me, or destroy me. I don't give him that power. Jesus said that NOTHING shall by any means hurt me! How about you?

CHAPTER 4
I Shall Not Want

In this chapter, I'm going to zero in on the word *WANT*.

The Shorter Oxford English Dictionary definition of the word *want* is the following:

Want (wont), v. M.E. [- O.N. *vanta* be lacking, lack: cf. prec. and Wane v.] **1.** *intr.* To be lacking or missing; not to be forthcoming; to be deficient in quantity or degree. **b.** To be lacking to complete a certain total or achieve a result. Const. *of* or with neg. clause. -1768. **2.** *trans.* To lack; to be destitute of or deficient in. Now *rare*, exc. with obj. a desirable quality or attribute. M.E. **b.** To come short by (so much) of completing a certain total or attaining a certain result. **c.** To be deprived of, to lose - 1724. **d.** *Wanting*: deprived of, without; lacking, less, minus. **e.** To go or do without.

I could continue with this definition, but there is enough there to get the proper meaning. Read aloud right now the above definition of the word *want* to yourself.

As I talked about the English language, I made the comment that we were taught to talk wrong. It's been about this word *want*.

Let me give you some illustrations of things people say:

"I want God to bless me."
"I want to have a happy life."

The preacher will ask:
"How many here want God to move in their lives?"
(Everyone raises their hand to say yes.)

"I don't want to get a divorce."
"We want revival to come in our church."
"I want a wife
"I want to get out of debt."
"I want more time with my family."
"I don't want my children to get hurt."
"I don't want to lose my job."
"I want my business to grow."

We have often prayed in agreement with one another about these things (according to Matthew 18:19). We have confessed we will have what we say and get happy. But later, we wonder what is going on. Why aren't these things happening? Did we understand what we confessed and prayed?

Isaiah 55:11
> So shall my word be that goeth forth out of my mouth: it shall not return unto me void, but it shall accomplish that which I please, and it shall prosper *in the thing* whereto I sent it.

We've confessed and claimed that verse for all the words we have spoken too. So why are we not getting the results we have expected? We are truly getting what we are saying, but as I shall show you, we did not know what was really being spoken by our mouths.

I trust the following will alarm you as it did me. What are we saying when we use the phrase "I want"? It is a confession. As the dictionary says, *want* refers to lack. There is no meaning for *want* other than lack and poverty. As you may check for yourself, every reference to *want* in the entire Bible refers to lack, destitution, and poverty. *Want* does *not* mean desire. That has been the lie and deception.

I have checked out other Bible translations where *want* was properly translated as lack. On the other hand, I have also come across Bibles where *want* was translated and used in an erroneous fashion, saying that Jesus wants, or wanted. Here's a fact: Jesus never wanted for anything! I leave it up to you to decide what should be done with that Bible. Feel free to discard it. A Bible translated in error can be misleading. Remember, one error in a math calculation can cause a ripple effect in subsequent calculations. Such is the case with erroneous information in your mind. Even modern-day dictionaries define *want* to equal *desire* and *desire* to equal *want*. That's confusion. They didn't equal before, and they still don't.

When I first had this revelation, out of curiosity I went around interviewing people to see what they thought the word *want* meant. I got all kinds of answers from people. Nobody seemed to really know.

Let's look at the illustrations I used just a while ago and see what those statements really are saying!

"I am deficient in and lack God to bless me."

"I lack and come short of having a happy life."

"I am more deficient in time with my family."

(North Americans take the fewest vacations, work longer hours than any other nation on earth, live in the most prosperous nation on earth, yet according to the Social Security Administration 98% of Americans are either dead or broke by the age of 65. Only 2% of Americans are financially stable at 65. What have we been claiming with our mouths? And are we enjoying life?)

The preacher is asking:
"How many are lacking and going without God moving in their lives?" (Everyone raises his or her hand in the affirmative.)

The spouse whose husband or wife is leaving them against their desires says:

"I don't lack and will not be deprived of getting a divorce." (She or he is confessing the exact opposite of what her or his heart desires.)

"We lack revival in our church."

"I lack and am going without having a wife (or husband.)"

41

This next one is a big one:
"I lack and am deprived of and will go ill-provided for to get out of debt."

(Basically, the one making this statement is saying "I am staying in debt.")

"I do not lack and will not be deprived of losing my job."

"I lack and am deprived of my business growing."

"I do not lack and am not deprived of my children getting hurt." Basically, the person is asking for hurt to come to their children.

For singles:
"I am deprived of having a wife (or husband)," or I want a wife (or husband.)

This is what we have been confessing! You may come back and say to me: "Oh yes, but God knows what I mean when I say those things." He sure does! But you don't!

Or you may say: "But God knows what I'm saying in my heart. He knows my heart." God always knows your heart, but it's your words that the angels are watching over to perform, not your heart. And words don't change meaning. If words changed meaning, then who would know what I'm saying here? Right?!!

Psalm 103:20
    Bless the LORD, ye his angels, that excel in strength, that do his commandments, hearkening unto the voice of his word.

HIS Word. God's Word coming out of your mouth. Jesus said you will have whatsoever you say, not whatsoever you mean! Remember, you have heard it often that if you don't like the world you've been living in, then change the words you've been saying. You've done that, but has anything really changed dramatically? You were not told that some words meant the exact opposite of what you were trained to think they mean!

"The gospel means good news. That means, poor man, you don't have to be poor no more."

I agreed when I heard that statement. And in my mind, I was left with the question: How? The above statement is true. The gospel is good news, and poor man, you don't have to be poor no more.

But how? Glory to God! He has shown us how! ***I shall not want!***

Remember, the world you live in was created by the words you spoke yesterday. Look around you and review what you have been saying, and think about how many times you have spoken the word *want*. Ask the Holy Spirit to revive your memory and show you instances where you used the word "want", and also to show you the results of those words. Look around you at the evidence that is already in your life to judge this truth. Did you get your heart's desires? I pray right now that the Holy Spirit opens your eyes and shows you the evidence of this truth.

I'm asking you to do this because that's exactly what I asked the Holy Spirit to do. See, truth was truth before I knew it, and if this word *want* meant poverty before, the results should confirm this. It was like a Rolodex of memories that came flooding in, and God showed me the times when I used the word *want* and the results of those confessions. Want produced poverty in my life.

One saying at church I used to always hear from other youth was: "Don't tell God that you don't want to go to Africa, because then God will send you there." (Do you see what was actually spoken?) I just kept my mouth shut and didn't say a word! Going to Africa is not a bad thing, but I had no desire to go there at all. As for the people who said that they didn't want to go to Africa, and then went, it wasn't God who sent them, their words took them. Because in reality they confessed, "I do not lack and will not go without and will not be deprived of going to Africa." The finances for their trip to Africa were released because they spoke out, "I don't want," and even took it as a sign of confirmation that they were supposed to go as the money came in! I'm telling you, this four-letter word *want* is a powerful word, and a very misunderstood word.

My friends were observing something they couldn't quite put their finger on. They were watching people go to Africa after saying, "I don't want to go," knowing they had no desire in their heart to go.

The devil has had people in darkness about this, and he loves people to use this word because they loose his power to work against them. God is a good God, and gives us the desires of our hearts. So why would God *make* someone go to Africa if they didn't desire to go? Well, He didn't; they did.

Proverbs 6:2
   Thou art snared with the words of thy mouth, thou art taken with the words of thy mouth.

Let me hit you with the definition of *want* again, this time from the Hebrew dictionary.

Want (from chacer) a prim. root, to lack; by impl. to *fail*, want, lessen, be abated, bereave, decrease, (cause to) fail, (have) lack, make lower, want.

That is it. There are no extra meanings! I pray that this next statement really shocks you, as it did me.

The word *need* is defined as *extreme want!!*

And we have confessed that we need this and we need that and also that we do not need this, all along using the word *need*, thinking it means: desire to have, will get, or must have. In Philippians 4:19 Paul wrote, "God shall supply all your need according to His riches in glory by Christ Jesus."

Therefore, you will never need. But if you keep confessing that you need, then you will need. Get it?

Psalm 107:2
    Let the redeemed of the LORD say *so*, *whom* he hath redeemed from the hand of the enemy.

Listen: **Jesus Redeemed Us from Want.**

So you might ask me: "How do we talk then?" Let's look to Jesus. Jesus said to blind Bartimaeus:

Mark 10:51
> What wilt thou that I should do unto thee?

Jesus didn't say, "what do you want Me to do for you?"! Maybe in some modern-day translation, but that is error. I have gotten rid of some Bibles that are in error.

Since that eventful day when the Holy Spirit spoke to Kay, I have dramatically changed the words and the way I speak. Here are ways to avoid using *want* and *need* the *wrong* way.

Where we used *want*, we should use:
- would like
- desire
- do not want

Where we used *need*, we should use:
- must, require
- have got to
- have to, will not *or* do not need

The word *want* is in the Bible over 55 times, and not one time does *want* mean desire. Let us look at some verses where it is used.

Psalm 34:9-10
O fear the LORD, ye his saints: for *there is* no want to them that fear him.
The young lions do lack, and suffer hunger: but they that seek the LORD shall not want any good *thing.*

Judges 18:10
When ye go, ye shall come unto a people secure, and to a large land: for God hath given it into your hands; a place where *there is* no want of any thing that *is* in the earth.

Psalm 23:1
The LORD *is* my shepherd; I shall not want.

Proverbs 21:5
The thoughts of the diligent *tend* only to plenteousness; but of every one *that is* hasty only to want.

This is where the mind gets renewed and we learn to talk right. Go back to these four verses you just read and substitute the word *want* for *desire.* This is what we've been trained to think *want* means. So now, doing this, do any of these verses make sense?

God's way is foolishness to the natural mind. What

are you saying when you say: "I do not want___"? You are saying: "I do not have a lack of, deficiency of, or poverty of or for (you name it)." Remember! We get what we say!

Taking the former examples,

- we say: "I want God to bless me." We should be saying: "I do not want God to bless me."

- we say: "I want to have a happy life." We should be saying: "I do not want to have a happy life."

- the preacher should ask: "How many people do not want for (as in lack) God to move in their lives?!" (The hands should now be raised.)

- we say: "We want revival to come to our church." We should be saying: "We do not want revival to come to our church."

- a spouse says: "I don't want a divorce." She or he should be saying: "I do want a divorce." (Wouldn't that shock the other spouse who does not have this revelation!) And besides, you are also confessing that "you are deprived of getting a divorce" (your heart's desire).

- we say: "I want more time with my wife and family." We should be saying: "I do not want more time with my wife (or husband) and family."

- we say: "I want a wife (or husband)." We should be saying: "I do not want a wife (or husband)."

This next one sounds really crazy to the natural mind.

- we say: "I want to get out of debt." We should be saying: "I do not want to get out of debt."

- we say: "I do not want to lose my job." We should be saying: "I want to lose my job," or "I will not lose my job."

Want does not mean desire! Want has nothing to do with desire. Want is poverty. Want is a negative. Confess the above "not wants" with your mouth and watch the Lord start to change your world! Hallelujah! You will be changing the direction of the rudder of your ship and your ship will turn! Remember, your tongue is the rudder of your ship, and by using this word *want* the wrong way, your ship has been headed south, when you thought it was headed north.

This is why the poor man does not have to be poor anymore. He can cancel out poverty and lack with this in his mouth: *"I shall not want."*

With this word *want* being used so frequently in our mouths, the devil has had a heyday in our lives. His day is over! I've stopped him. Will you? That *want* fire that has been coming from your tongue has been burning up the prosperity and abundant life God came to give, and for which your heart yearns.

If your brain is screaming at you right now, know this: The battle the devil wages against you occurs in your mind. Your tongue is connected to your brain. This "not want" stuff may seem wrong to you, but Wisdom says:

Proverbs 16:25
   There is a way that seemeth right unto a man; but the end thereof *are* the ways of death.

Proverbs 1:23(a)
   Turn you at my reproof. (Wisdom is talking.)

Have you been unknowingly kicking life into the devil with your mouth so he can work against you? The following is a quote from a preacher I once heard:

"The battle cannot continue if you stop kicking life into him (the devil). Saint of God, WAKE UP! The foe is defeated! The truth of the matter is the battle is in your mind. As long as you think that satan is mighty and powerful, he can hurt you."

You kick life into the devil with your words.

Want has led you captive.

Philippians 4:19
But my God shall supply all your need according to his riches in glory by Christ Jesus.

From this statement, God has taken care of need. Jesus has supplied everything. He is our source. Just one verse back, Paul said: "I have all, and abound: I am full." Look at this next verse. This is rich.

2 Peter 1:3
According as his divine power hath given unto us all things that *pertain* unto life and godliness, through the knowledge of him that hath called us to glory and virtue…

Ephesians 1:3
Blessed *be* the God and Father of our Lord Jesus Christ, who hath blessed us with all spiritual blessings in heavenly *places* in Christ.

"Hath blessed" means He has already done it.

Psalm 37:4
Delight thyself also in the LORD; and he shall give thee the desires of thine heart.

Proverbs 10:24(b)
But the desire of the righteous shall be granted.

Psalm 3:8(b)
Thy blessing *is* upon thy people.

Proverbs 10:22
The blessing of the LORD, it maketh rich, and he addeth no sorrow with it.

Proverbs 12:13-14(a)
The wicked is snared by the transgression of *his* lips: but the just shall come out of trouble.
A man shall be satisfied with good by the fruit of *his* mouth.

Does that fire you up?

The power of saying that you "do not want __"

appears to push open the doors and blow away obstacles like dynamite to allow you to go in that direction! In the direction of what you say "you do not want"! Powerful!

That's why people have been struggling. They're putting obstacles in their own paths that have been stopping them from getting what their hearts desire by cursing themselves with want (poverty).

How about this confession? "I just want to spend more time with my spouse. I don't want him or her to be gone all the time. He really does want to spend more time with the children, don't you know!" Those are bad confessions if time with your family is your heart's desire.

"If you want something you never had, you have to do something you never did." This is the talk we have been used to. We have been programmed to think *want* means "desire". It doesn't.

God is a good God. He's not holding back our desires. We've been doing that! Look at the following verse that Paul wrote:

Romans 7:19-20
For the good that I would, I do not: but the evil which I would not, that I do.
Now if I do that I would not, it is no more I that do it, but sin that dwelleth in me.

If there was ever a place in the Bible where the word *want* could have been used as we have been taught to think it means, it would have been here in Paul's writings. Paul didn't say, "For the good that I want to do I do not." They had the word *want* back in those days. They, however, were taught to use it properly, because they knew what it meant.

God has called us out of darkness into the kingdom of light, and He will restore the years that the locust has eaten. Glory to God!! He is for us. But we must line up our words with His to allow His salvation to flow.

You were taken captive by your words and your worlds were formed. Words ensnared you, but words directed by the Holy Spirit will un-snare you. God delivers you from the snare of the fowler. God is waiting to give you a new life, one that He even has given you the desires for, but your words have been stout against Him. When you get in line with God's Word, and speak like He does, His power flows.

Remember Kay? God showed me how powerful that word *want* was in her case. When I came up to the house after cutting the lawn mower off, the very first words she said were:

"I don't *want* you to pray for me; I *want* to go and kill myself." She was serious. But she thought she was saying: "I don't desire you to pray for me; I desire to kill myself."

Now, did Kay get what she said, or did she get what she thought she was saying and what her heart desired? She said she didn't want (or lack) us to pray for her. Kay's words loosed God's power, which blew away obstacles that might have prevented us from praying for her, and actually also caused us to pray. In less than a minute we were praying for her, and she didn't kill herself. She got exactly what she said. Her own words kept her alive and opened the doors for us to pray, because she used the word *want*. Are you seeing this? Kay did not get her heart's desire of liking to kill herself either. Saying she wanted to kill herself loosed the obstacles into her own path that stopped her from going any further down that road to suicide.

This is a revision of my first printing, and since then I have seen this revelation proved over and over in the lives of many other people.

Think about people you have heard say, "I don't want to be a Christian." What happened to them? One of the people God brought to my remembrance was an atheist I knew in university. He told me at the time that he didn't "want to be a Christian." I was a bit shocked and didn't say anything to him. I was thinking that he said he had "absolutely no desire to be a Christian." Two years later, I met him in an airport, and by that time he had become a Christian. I thought at the time, "Wow, how did that happen?" but now I know that his own words took him through the circumstances to become a Christian.

Could it really be this simple? Could the whole world be deceived about this word *want* and no one has discovered this before? Could just changing the way we use this word really change anything? The Bible supports an answer of *yes*! I asked myself these same questions. And it is that simple.

Is this legalism? Legalism is defined as being strict, often too strict and literal, or as adherence to law. Well, shouldn't we take the Bible literally and adhere to God's law? Don't we do that with Romans 10:9 and 10 concerning salvation?

> *Romans 10:9-10*
> That if thou shalt confess with thy mouth the Lord Jesus, and shalt believe in thine heart that God hath raised him from the dead, thou shalt be saved.
> For with the heart man believeth unto righteousness; and with the mouth confession is made unto salvation.

While I was first writing this book, there was a war going on in my mind and I questioned this revelation numerous times. But I kept coming to the conclusion that this is truth. I had the proof. God showed me that the things I said I did not want, I got, and the things I said that I wanted, I didn't get.

This universe was set up to operate on words, and *want* has never ceased meaning poverty, and *want*, when spoken, has never ceased producing poverty.

If you look at Psalm 23:1, you can see now that this is a double negative statement. *Not* is negative, and now you understand that *want* is a negative. What do two negatives make? An absolute positive.

In the book of Luke, Jesus was talking with the disciples, and in my opinion the disciples were complaining to Jesus. At the Last Supper, when Jesus was talking with His disciples after the meal, He asked them a question.

Luke 22:35
And he said unto them, When I sent you without purse, and scrip, and shoes, lacked ye any thing? And they said, Nothing.

They lacked nothing!

CHAPTER 5
The Land of No Want

Eat up the following verse:

1 Corinthians 1:28
And base things of the world, and things which are despised, hath God chosen, *yea*, and things which are not, to bring to naught things that are.

There is a miracle in your mouth. Bring to nothing the things that *are*, by the words of your mouth and the word *want*.

Deuteronomy 30:11-14
For this commandment which I command thee this day, it *is* not hidden from thee, neither *is* it far off.

It *is* not in heaven, that thou shouldest say, Who shall go up for us to heaven, and bring it unto us, that we may hear it, and do it?

Neither *is* it beyond the sea, that thou shouldest

say, Who shall go over the sea for us, and bring it unto us, that we may hear it, and do it?

But the word *is* very nigh unto thee, in thy mouth, and in thy heart, that thou mayest do it.

The Land of No Want is in your mouth, in the words that you say. God is watching over His Word to perform it. The angels are waiting to carry out His Word when it is spoken out of your mouth. When the word *want* came out of your mouth in ignorance of its true meaning, it too was acted upon, but not necessarily by the angels, and it created poverty in the area about which you spoke.

Judges 18:10

When ye go, ye shall come unto a people secure, and to a large land: for God hath given it into your hands; a place where *there is* no want of any thing that *is* in the earth.

This Land of No Want is a large land, a place where you have everything. "Thy will be done, on earth as it is in heaven." There is no want in heaven.

Do you want heaven on earth? Watch your answer.

Warning:

Your brain will scream at you and tell you this is wrong.

Answer:

Smash your brain with God's Word coming out of your mouth: *I shall not want!*

If you are not convinced yet, have a look at the definition of *poverty.*

From the Shorter Oxford English Dictionary:

Poverty (po verti). The quality or condition of being poor. 1. The condition of having little or no wealth or material possessions; indigence, destitution, want (in various degrees). b. *fig.* in allusion to *Matt.* 5:3. M.E. c. Personified and applied to a person, or persons. II. 1. Deficiency, dearth, scarcity; smallness of amount. etc......

Are you seeing it? The definitions of *want* and of poverty are basically the same. It's shocking. *Desire* doesn't mean want or poverty. The definitions of these words haven't suddenly changed. We have believed for prosperity, but have been confessing want and poverty. Lack has been our confession. And the devil's power was loosed to cause poverty to appear. No wonder people continue in the rat race and have no time to do anything or enjoy life! They've been snared by the words of their mouths and this four-letter word!

Disease is defined as the absence of ease. How many of you want ease in your finances?

If you said yes to that question, go back and read this book again. The answer to that question is No. You do not *want* ease in your finances anymore. Jesus bore all of our diseases on Calvary, and if He bore them, then we don't have to bear them. Glory to God!!

Are you going to start talking different? Good. That was my intent for this book.

After a lifetime of using this word the wrong way, and thinking it was the truth, it will take some effort to get used to it. But truth is always truth. Truth never changes, and truth never lies. No matter how much we may deny truth, it doesn't change. And truth is no respecter of persons.

Before I knew about this revelation, I had a desire to get married, but was saying, "I want to get married." This confession is translated: "I lack and will go without getting married." In the past I had met a nice girl, but I confessed with my mouth that I wanted to marry her. I got exactly what I confessed, which was the opposite of what my heart desired. Basically, no matter how much I tried to make it happen, I sentenced myself to being single with my mouth and that word *want*. I put obstacles and hindrances in my own way.

So the very first thing I confessed out of my mouth that morning I had the call from Kay was these words: "Father, I do not want to get married anymore." I had a physical sensation of weight being lifted off my shoulders. A very unique thing happened that morning too. All the anxiety about getting married left me, and five months later I met a wonderful girl whom I would eventually marry. I was 31.

Years ago back in Canada, I was applying to go back to university. A few professors were reviewing my application, and I did not know when or if I was going to be accepted. I went back to my hometown for a week's visit while working out west. I was trying to finalize my plans during this week, and after a lot of running around, I prayed. I said to the Lord, "If You don't want me to go back to university, then I don't want to go back." I thought I was surrendering to God, being spiritual, or that sort of thing. I was thinking maybe it wasn't God's will for me to go back to university. I was also tired of trying to make it happen and I just gave up. But do you see what I confessed? I tapped into this word *want* and used it correctly for what my heart desired!

I'm telling you this story because, having no knowledge of what this word *want* meant, as soon as I spoke that prayer, I had a physical sensation of weight being lifted off my shoulders. This was the first time I ever experienced this feeling. And by now you should already know what happened. The next morning there was a nice heavy snow coming down, and my mother warned me to stay home. But I went to the school, and you guessed it, that morning I was accepted back to university.

I've only had the sensation of weight being lifted off my shoulders twice in my life. I'm not saying that you should expect this to happen to you, because as believers, signs follow us, we don't follow signs, and faith is not based on feelings. But in both instances, whether I understood what was said or not, the doors were opened in the direction of "I don't want ___."
I'm giving you examples from my life, but I am not alone in my experience with this word. Since 1993 I have watched and interviewed people and analyzed their use of this word *want*. Results have been consistent with what the Holy Spirit has revealed to me. When someone *thinks* he's saying "I don't desire something," he gets the *something* he said he *did not want*. I almost feel like I've been doing a lab experiment all these years.

You will find our society well trained in confessing and using the word *want* (poverty). If you go to a fast-food outlet, the attendant may ask you, "do you want fries with that?" Now when you say yes, you *will* get the fries. Being trained that using the word *want* in this instance gets what we desire in these small examples has made us think that this word means "desire," or "would like to have." The usage of the word *want* has changed just like the usage of the word *gay*. People understand it and use it that way. But as mentioned before, just because the use is different doesn't change the true meaning of the word.

After I realized what *want* meant, I trained myself to answer a question like the one above with: "I will have the fries," thus avoiding to accept or answer the question "Do you want ___" with a yes. Or I would sometimes say: "No, I don't want the fries, I would like the fries." The attendant would look at me funny. And as I said, it took me two weeks to break this word off my tongue and use it correctly. Why was I so adamant about these little things? Because I was retraining myself to speak correctly and get what my heart desired when it came to the big issues of life, like getting married. I saw the results of my own confessions from the past, and was in a hurry to change the direction of my ship. And I wasn't worried if anyone thought I sounded crazy.

This brings up an observation, however, which I find interesting. No matter what my answer to the attendant about the "fries with that" question, I would get the fries. The attendant knows that it's my desire to have the fries and gives them to me. We were both talking in error. So what's happening here? People have been getting fries after saying yes to that question all the time. What's going on? Am I wrong about *want*? After conversations with Bible scholars and study, there is an issue of dominion and authority. I can say that I want to pick up a pen all day long, yet I can reach over with my arm and pick it up. I can say that I want to tell you something and proceed to tell you. I have control over my body because God has given me that authority in my body. But this is the limit. I can say that I want to drive across town and jump into my car, but I have just loosed obstacles in my own path to getting across town. Now, I will get across town if I never give up, but how long will it take? I cursed myself. Remember, *want* has never ceased meaning poverty.

I have experimented with this word numerous times. One test I like doing is the traffic test. Kay and I were in traffic on our way to Washington, D.C. one day, and we were in a traffic jam that seemed to go on for a mile. I turned to Kay and said, "Kay, I don't want this traffic to break up and dissolve, and I don't want to get through this traffic fast." Almost instantly we started to move and never slowed down, but kept moving, and the line-up seemed to dissolve before us. I've done this test numerous times. Angels come for my words.

When I left Canada for the U.S., I was sitting in my mom's kitchen reading a Christian magazine about a well known preacher who had been in Richmond, Virginia. All I could remember about Virginia was an article in *National Geographic* on Newport News shipbuilding. So I asked my mom, "What's in Virginia?" She answered: "Ah, Mike, you don't want to go there; there's nothing in Virginia." I agreed and said, "You're right Mom, I don't want to go there; I want to go to Texas." So I headed down to the States and stayed with relatives in Ohio. I then headed south and west to Texas, because in my mind, I was headed to Texas. Well, when I traveled just west of Interstate 75, I ran into a roadblock. Hundreds of other cars were parked on the highway with me and I had my engine turned off. I had driven all day and had gotten nowhere. Now, remember, I knew nothing about *want* or what it meant. And both my mom and I agreed together that I did not *want* to go to Virginia.

Matthew 18:19

Again I say unto you, That if two of you shall agree on earth as touching any thing that they shall ask, it shall be done for them of my Father which is in heaven.

That agreement about not wanting to go to Virginia and wanting to go to Texas made with my mother in her kitchen that day brought obstacles and roadblocks into my path to Texas, but cleared the way for me to go to Virginia. I had no clue what was being spoken out of my mouth. I ended up in Virginia.

Here are the experiences of some well-known preachers I highly respect and have listened to on many occasions. I think you will find them very interesting.

Norvel Hayes kept telling the Lord he didn't want to live anymore. Today, he's rich, free, and very much alive.

Morris Cerullo didn't want to be an evangelist; he wanted to be a lawyer. He's an evangelist.

R. W. Schambach didn't want to be a preacher; he left for the navy, and started preaching to others on the ships! He's my favorite preacher!

What about your favorite song at church? Do you really want to be like Jesus? Huh? Do you wanna? Do you want to see Him lifted up? Do you?

When I hear songs like this one being sung in church, with the word *want* being used incorrectly, I get a sick feeling in my stomach. It grieves my spirit.

Now, the following statements can be made that will result in your heart's desires coming to pass, even though it still may sound crazy to your brain.

- I do not want my children to be happy.
- I do not want money. I do not need money.
- I do not want success. I do not want wealth.
- I do not want God's best.
- I do not want God's direction.
- I do not want to go Diamond.
- I do not want to live life in abundance.
- I do not want lots of cash.
- I do not want all things supplied that pertain unto life and godliness.
- I do not want comfort and security.
- The blessing of the Lord is upon me and it makes me rich, and He adds no sorrow with it.
- I delight myself in the Lord and He gives me the desires of my heart.
- I do not want for anything good anymore.

Start today to undo what you have been saying and watch the yokes just break and fall away. Following is a prayer that I have written out for you to usher you into the Land of No Want:

"Father, I thank You for sending Your Son Jesus to die on the cross for me. I ask You Jesus, to forgive me of my sins; come into my heart, and be my Savior. Thank You, Jesus, that You have redeemed me from want, You have redeemed me from poverty, You have redeemed me from lack, You have redeemed me from loneliness, You have redeemed me from death, and You have redeemed me from hell. You didn't come to condemn me, but You came to set me free and that I might have life and have it more abundantly and extravagantly. I ask You to give me the abundant life You came to give. I do not want that abundant life anymore. Thank You, Jesus, that You have already supplied all my need. Now I do not need because You supply everything for me. Jesus, lead me into the Land of No Want so I may live there. Thank You, Jesus, for loving me and not giving up on me. Thank You. Amen."

CHAPTER 6

Romans 4:17

Romans 4:17

(As it is written, I have made thee a father of many nations,) before him whom he believed, *even* God, who quickeneth the dead, and calleth those things which be not as though they were.

On reading the New Testament years ago, I remember stumbling across this verse and being puzzled by it. I remember looking at this verse and not knowing how to understand it or apply it. Then a book came out called *The Fourth Dimension* in which Pastor Paul Cho brought this verse to light.

Calling those things which be not as though they were, is an act of faith. Faith is Now. Faith sees the physically unseen. Faith comes by hearing God's Word. And when we call something done when in the

physical realm it's not done, that is faith. And that is
how we please God. God spoke the words "Let there
be light" when it was totally dark. Then what happened?

So when you confess that you do not want money
when your wallet is empty, that's faith. When you
say that you do not want money (you do not lack or
are not deprived or impoverished of it), when your
bank and wallet say you have no money, you are
speaking in faith, and that pleases God. The rudder of
your ship has turned and things will start to change.
Circumstances and opportunities will align themselves
because of your words and will cause money to start
coming. But what have you been saying when your
wallet has been empty? Have you been saying to God:
"God, You know I want money. I need some money,
Lord. Please, I want some money." What did you
speak just then? All you did was confess to God that
you are poor. You thought you were asking Him for
money, didn't you? And that He was going to pour
money into your pockets too? But that didn't happen,
did it? Because that isn't asking God anything or telling Him anything that isn't already so. Nor was anything spoken in faith that would loose His power to
work for you. It was actually a confession for just the

opposite of what your heart desired. God moves when He sees our faith. You confessed a lack of money.

We were trained to talk wrong and use the word *want* in the wrong way. Money didn't come to us the way we desired it to. The devil jumped in on that little game in our mind and sometimes managed to get us to believe that maybe it wasn't God's will for us to have money, maybe God's desires are for us to be poor, because maybe our selfish desires of liking to pay our bills off are not what God desires. Maybe God is trying to teach us something through this poverty. Can God really trust us with money anyhow? Blah, blah, blah. All these are lies. You were talking wrong and not speaking faith! And you were getting the true results and fruit from that word *want*.

Have there been other lies, too, that may have been lingering in your mind? Such as, "If God desired me to be rich, then I would already be rich." Doesn't it seem logical that you would think like this, especially if you've been a Christian for a long time, have been believing God for wealth, and still have not seen riches come your way? You would put it over on God as if it's His fault, that He really doesn't like you to be rich or have money.

Why am I stressing money in this section? Well, for far too long wealth has been in the hands of the ungodly, and not in the hands of the righteous. If God can't trust you with money as you may have thought, then why does He trust a drug dealer who has thousands of dollars in his pocket? Is a drug dealer working for the Lord? Some Christians have been duped into believing that money is bad for them: that they might fall away from God if they had more money, and that they might go to hell for it. Listen, if that is true, then why isn't the devil just dumping tens of thousands of dollars into your lap to make it happen? I'll tell you why: It's a religious lie that has been keeping you broke! It's not true!

I love what Mike Murdock once said: "Money only magnifies a person. If they are evil, they will be more evil, and if they are good, they will be more good." It's the love of money that's bad, and you can have that even if you only have a penny to your name. The love of money is not dependent upon how much money you have. I also like what Norvel Hayes once said: "A poor man can't feed many people." Who said God can't trust you with money anyhow? God can't trust that drug dealer, so what does trust have to do with it really? What are you doing with the money you have right now? You probably have a lot more money today than you had ten years ago. Have you drifted away from the Lord because you have more money? And besides, that drug dealer was in business providing a product where there was a demand. Yes, it's drugs and it's a criminal activity, but I'm trying to shock your thinking out of believing that you are stuck with being broke.

That's why I got angry at the devil when I understood this revelation, and *unplugged* him from my life. I understood I was actually cursing myself and creating poverty in my life by the way I was using the word *want*. I did not see that before. Now, since having reversed the way I use that word, I am creating and commanding *prosperity* and *abundance* into my life. And like I said, even though I would get fries at a fast food restaurant, I was determined to reprogram the way I spoke when it came to the big issues of life that were not in my domain and out of my control.

A curse is created by words, and it causes bad things to happen. There is something about a curse, too, that no matter how much effort and energy in the physical you may exert to overcome it, you can't. You have to cancel it with your mouth in the name of Jesus and/or start confessing blessings. "Curse of poverty, I cancel you in the name of Jesus," is an example of how to do this. Go ahead and cancel all of the *bad* things you said *you don't want to happen* in your life.

Let me give you an instance from my life again. Just a week after this book was written, I was driving out into the country to where I was staying and my car ran out of gas. I was broke. At that time I was unemployed and seeking employment, and was low on cash ... very low on cash (a world created by my own mouth). So, I pulled off the road at an intersection with a gravel road. I got out of my car, and started to laugh. I opened the gas tank, put the gas cap on the fender, and was totally at peace. It was dusk and the bugs were coming out, and in Virginia the bugs are big. I spoke to the devil and said: **"You're a liar, devil, and you can't steal this revelation from me just because of an empty tank of gas. You see, *I don't want any gas for my car anymore, devil!!*"** I was loud. I prayed for gas and was in a surprisingly happy mood. I was laughing because I realized that I will never be without gas for my car ever again. How? Because I was calling those things which be not as though they were. I was speaking into existence that which was *not*. I was loosing God's creative power, providing power, supplying power, wealth-creating power, lack-destroying power by the words of *my* mouth and that word *want* to cause me to be in a place where I'll always be supplied with gas for my car, and I totally understood it.

Can you guess what happened? Less than an hour had gone by while I was out in the country when a pickup truck stopped. I wasn't advertising that I was out of gas or had my thumb stuck out to passers-by. I was standing off a ways from my car. The man got out and poured a gallon of gas into my car. I said, "I can't pay you because I have no money." He said, "No problem." I thanked him and headed on down the road, laughing all the way. I've never been without gas or money for gas since.

Are you seeing this? We have more control than we ever thought we had. This four-letter word **want** has been creating undesirable results, making us think that words are not powerful, and even that God was against us.

I never knew how programmed human beings could get until I tried to change my speech. It's like a tire in a rut. Trying to get it out takes a lot of effort since it likes to stay in the rut! Saying "I don't want money" may sound strange to you if you've never heard this before, but after more than a decade of talking this way, it's normal for me. But having lots of money is also normal for me now.

Have you ever watched a flock of birds in the air while they were flying? When the whole flock changed direction, have you ever looked for the leader? You could't really see who it was, could you? But then the flock changed direction again and again, and no single bird seemed to be leading! What was happening? All that the birds were doing was watching their neighbors. When their neighbors changed direction, they changed direction. No one was leading. That's what happens with society. People do what everyone else does. It's a fight to break out of the norm. And it's also a fight to change the way you speak.

People move in the same direction as their neighbors and speak the same words. But hear what the rich say. What do they say? They say, "I don't need any money. I don't want money." The rich get richer and the poor get poorer. I challenge you to start using the word *want* correctly and start calling those things which be not as though they were. This is not magic, but one of God's powerful laws that work.

Let's go a little deeper here. Let me ask you a question. What would happen if every Christian in America started confessing that they *don't want* to win people to Jesus anymore, that they don't *want* God back in America, that they don't *want* Him to move more than ever before, and that they don't *want* their unsaved friends and family to come to Jesus? Would revival break out? I believe that this would turn this nation upside down!

CHAPTER 7

Other Words, Nuggets, and Psalm 23

At this point you may not be surprised to hear that there are other words that are being used incorrectly in our society as well.

Nugget 1

Take *care*! This has become almost the standard farewell in America today... But let's see what this word *care* means.

Care (kar), n. [A.S. caru, sorrow], 1. Mental pain; worry; anxiety. 2. Close attention; watchfulness; heed. 5. Something to worry about, watch over, or attend to.

Jesus' reply to Martha:

Luke 10:41

And Jesus answered and said unto her, Martha, Martha, thou art careful and troubled about many things.

1 Peter 5:7

Casting all your care upon him; for he careth for you.

Philippians 4:6-7

Be careful for nothing; but in every thing by prayer and supplication with thanksgiving let your requests be made known unto God.

And the peace of God, which passeth all understanding, shall keep your hearts and minds through Christ Jesus.

The two words *careful* and *care* have the same root meaning. Obviously, Jesus was telling Martha that being careful was *not* a good thing.

I have always watched myself and never used the word *care* at all since I heard a well-known preacher say that when you hear the world using a phrase or an expression, beware: as in *take care*.

So about a year ago, I was trying to accomplish a great task I had been believing for and had flown across the country to finish. I was confessing that I did not want it to happen, but I still was unable to finish that goal then. I had my rudder turned in the right direction using the word *want* correctly, but my ship was not entering port that day. I came out of the building we were in and I said to my wife, "I don't care if I ever get this done." Well, I'm telling you, the moment I said that I felt like rubber bands started snapping off my head. I just confessed I don't have any mental pain or worry. I'd never seen this before then, but again we have been subliminally brainwashed here too to believe that *care* is synonymous with the word *love*. That if I say I don't care for someone, I'm saying I don't love that person. Not true. That day I kept saying over and over, "I don't care, I don't care, I don't care," and it felt so good, I kept on saying it all day. And for the first time in years I felt that peace that passes all understanding come all over me. It was God's peace. God showed me that *care* involves mental pain from asking those six questions: Who? What? Where? When? Why? and How? My brain was so overloaded on how I was going to accomplish this task that I was caring without even realizing it. Even feels good just writing this down.

I forgot about this goal, and within five months it was completed by someone I knew. Glory to God! Take care for nothing! Watch and pray!

Nugget 2

Here's a shocker. Do you know that song "I Surrender All"? Have you ever looked for the word *surrender* in the Bible? It's not there. *Surrender* is defined as giving up, as in being beaten in battle.

Surrender (sur-ren-der). 1. To give up possession of or power over. 2. To give up or abandon: as, to surrender all hope.

God never told us to surrender, yet we sing that song and think we're being spiritual. God told us to *submit* ourselves unto Him and resist the devil. My Bible tells me to stand and fight the good fight of faith, and then having done all to stand, keep standing. I believe we sang it because we were trying to figure out how to get God to work for us, and we saw something here.

Ephesians 6:13-14

Wherefore take unto you the whole armor of God, that ye may be able to withstand in the evil day, and having done all, to stand.

Stand therefore, having your loins girt about with truth, and having on the breastplate of righteousness.

1 Timothy 6:12

Fight the good fight of faith, lay hold on eternal life, whereunto thou art also called, and hast professed a good profession before many witnesses.

86

Nugget 3

How about *sorry*? Remember that verse that says the joy of the Lord is your strength? Here it is in full.

Nehemiah 8:10
Then he said unto them, Go your way, eat the fat, and drink the sweet, and send portions unto them for whom nothing is prepared: for *this* day is holy unto our Lord: neither be ye sorry; for the joy of the LORD is your strength.

Neither be ye sorry. Don't be sorry. Look at the definitions of *sorry* below. It has nothing to do with apologizing.

Sorry (sor'i), adj. [-RIER, -RIEST], [< A.S. sarig, in pain < *sar*, sore] 1. Full of sorrow, pity, or regret: as, we were sorry to leave. 2. Inferior in worth or quality; poor. 3. Wretched; dismal; pitiful.

Sorrow (sor'o), n. [< A.S. *sorg*] 1. Mental suffering caused by loss, disappointment, etc.; sadness; grief. 2. That which produces such suffering; trouble, etc. 3. The outward expression of such suffering; mourning. 4. The devil.

Say: "Forgive me," "Excuse me," "Pardon me," or "I apologize," rather than "I'm sorry." Don't confess that you're full of grief and despair.

Nugget 4

Incredible (in-kred-e-b'l) *adj.* Not credible; unbelievable; seeming too unusual or improbable to be possible.

Fantastic (fan-tas-tik), adj. [< O.Fr. < M.L. < L.L. < Gr. *phantastikos,* able to present to the mind < *phainein,* to show] 1. Imaginary; unreal: as, *fantastic* reasons. 2. Grotesque; odd; quaint: as, a *fantastic* hat. 3. Extravagant; capricious; eccentric.

Fabulous (fab'yoo-list), adj. [< L. < *fibula;* see FABLE] 1. Of or like a fable; imaginary; fictitious; legendary. 2. Incredible; astounding.

Are we quietly programming ourselves that nothing is believable and everything is unreal? Then, when we hear God's Word we doubt it? This is exposing the devil's tricks.

Let's look now at Psalm 23. Here it is in full.
Psalm 23
1. The LORD *is* my shepherd; I shall not want.
2. He maketh me to lie down in green pastures: he leadeth me beside the still waters.
3. He restoreth my soul: he leadeth me in the paths of righteousness for his name's sake.
4. Yea, though I walk through the valley of the shadow of death, I will fear no evil: for thou

art with me; thy rod and thy staff they comfort
me.

5. Thou preparest a table before me in the pres-
ence of mine enemies: thou anointest my head
with oil; my cup runneth over.

6. Surely goodness and mercy shall follow me all
the days of my life: and I will dwell in the house
of the LORD for ever.

I heard one time that there are so many sermons
contained in Psalm 23 you could preach and never
run out of material.

I would like you to think about this thought: Verse
one is written before all the other verses. Do you think
God knew in what order He would like these verses
written down? I'll leave you with a question to ask
yourself: In verse *five* your cup runs over. (*Cup* in
Hebrew is translated "a bag for money.") Do you think
that's dependant on verse *one* and *you not wanting?*

A last observation came to me over a year ago when
I was on a wave runner in Tennessee. I was in the
middle of the lake and looking all around, and the
Holy Spirit started talking to me. God loves this world
and made it with abundance. There's no lack of air,
no lack of trees, no lack of water, no lack of dirt.

There's actually an overabundance of those things, and yet how much more does God love us than the earth itself? Did He say, "I'll make the earth with abundance, but the humans I'll create with poverty?" NO! NO! NO!

When Jesus died on that cross, He crushed the devil. He bore our sicknesses and diseases AND He destroyed POVERTY. But our words must be in line and agree with His words to receive His promises. It's really easy. By His stripes we were healed, and we shall not want!

As a closing note, I'd like to say that since I first wrote this book in 1993, my life has totally changed. Businesses have sprung up, and I am never without money. I've been married now for years. And an interesting thing has happened. A friend in San Francisco asked me this question: "Michael, since you changed the way you use the word *want*, do you find that you have more peace in your life?" I paused and thought about that strange question. And not even realizing it, I was startled to see that I do have more peace than I ever had before. When you know that you'll never be without money, and I mean *never*. Because you confess, "I never want money anymore," you will have peace. What do you have to worry about? I unplugged the devil from my life and finances in 1993 by the words of my mouth, and the switch of want has long been shut off in my life. There were a few attacks because of this revelation. But I am never in want or need! I now use the word *want* the correct way. Psalm 23:1 "The Lord is my shepherd. *I shall not want.*"

I have one last question for you:

Do You Want to Be a Millionaire?

What is your final answer?